toy fabels

CASS McCOMBS

SPURL EDITIONS

WE MADE OUR MOPS

We made our mops out of crystal geyser bottles and a sponge
                    deco mops and wood stains
shoe polish containers, like the long necked ones
with the sponge on top
                    paint racked from flax or jobsites or some person's
                                              garage
                                    doesn't count otherwise.

however deviant, it's all a game
no way to justify except that I love to roam around at night
                    to places I shouldn't have been
muni yards and tunnels
    drunk   retarded
going over labored pieces as a gag
when the throwup emigrated west
the uglier and the bigger was the better.

I remember N Judah tunnel alone
rolled on by a rival crew
no coincidence they knew where to find me
somebody sold me out
    got my teeth kicked in.

I remember breaking my legs in chicago
    all these memories streaming
    from a hole in the back of my head

yet will all come around again like karma's scales
vandalism charges trials fines testimonies . . .
just like a freshly yellow painted wall
will be drawn over by the next kid
                whos tired of sanctioned psycho cities.

me I'm tired of beef and plebeian politics
get me high shut up or fight
    I saw a scaffolding I want to check out
    and a billboard
        by the Nimitz Freeway.

                There's the chance I won't make it back
so just in case – remember
    tell my family I love them

my friends can have all my notebooks
                              I have nothing else
throw my body off a cliff to be eaten by wild animals.

      just kidding. I don't care what happens to my body.

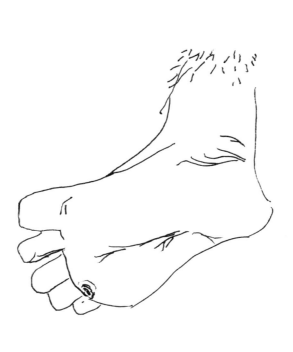

Warlocks of sf shared there daily meal atop metallic whale pelvisbone.
warlocks of nyc had yellow armpits from holy decadence of

                                          hang gliding.

warlocks of sf teased a dumpster sized bumble bee.
warlocks of nyc danced the balboa through an underwater pet hospital.
warlocks of sf racked ghost spunk to coat walls of there cryptwhite.
warlocks of nyc propelled subway train by chewing bitter dragon

                                                wing.

warlocks of sf ritually ate body of martinez joe dimaggio.
warlocks of nyc bleated a spurious tune.

VIOLENT STORY

Saw a guy get his ear ripped off with a hammer, these jocks came up from la like these corny kid rock jocks. some people are violent because that's what they do, these la jocks were violent because they thought that's what they had to do: kick the shit out of anyone who said anything about what they were doing, anyone perceived as blocking their way, random people like bus drivers. they pulled us out of a liquor store and tried to curb me, you know what that is? when they hold your teeth on the corner of a curb and kick down on the back of your head. it was halloween and these guys storm into the liquor store wearing scream masks, the kind of guys that wear scream masks, the whole store became one giant exploded glass bottle. then there were these hardcore punks, the corniest type of person, hardcore punks. they beat up randoms with a bike lock, shop owners, other writers, but this is all violence in sf, it wasn't like new york, they would definitely be glad to stab you there. new york has a whole history the west doesn't have, each letter a whole evolution to it. I have this friend from new york, his crew was his dad's crew.

five out of nine guys in my crew are dead now. two suicide, the murder, drugs and cancer.

TWO TYPES OF PEOPLE

Either you're the type of person
that prefers to believe in a world
where there was a Butthole Surfers
Electriclarryland billboard
up for almost a decade
in SF –
or you are not.

You say you never saw it,
but you forgot to mention:
You are blind.

People see
only what
they want
to see.

The
billboard
is
still
up.

TELEPATHY

Working on a wall,
    lights flash behind us.
I'm like – let's run!
He's like – that's not for us.

Police pull up directly across the street,
        begin talking to some junkies.
We calmly finish our work.
That's telepathy.

TAGGING A CHURCH

Tagging a church
obv not the most hidden spot
probably won't endear myself to the cops,
  who are probably already following me.
then why?
who is the largest owner of real estate of the world?
who takes money from the poor to buy real estate?
who institutionalizes violence toward children?
was I raised catholic?
I was raised nothing.

nevermind the false theology,
the heretic idea of an indoor god
and whatever it's not like I tagged the *inside* of a church.

  I had to run through all these thoughts first,
probably someone else would've just done it like it was anywhere else,
because it is.
I've tagged people's homes' front doors willynilly
windows of small shops owned by honest working class people
    I know I already caused alot of people to feel
violated.

part of this life is that it's not right,
or that there's parts of everyone's lives that is not right,
instead of pretending otherwise,

to put it out there,
in the open.

we start wars for oil and chop up children with daisycutter bombs and people
get enraged when property is vandalized?

maybe the least we can do is think and talk
about all these things and how fucked up everything is.
and I'm just like anyone else
I don't know what the answer is.

SOUTHBAY STYLE

Alot of people who are drawn into this life have a darkness, square people
don't like it and eventually that comes around to you, i'm not even talking
metaphysically, if you spend your time making things square people don't
like, square people don't like you and it eats at you. you read stuff like french
situationist text and that kind of thing and from that perspective, it's pure
because there's no money involved, it's not for sale. temporary. it's all about
domination. as far as throw ups, don't worry the vomit irony was not lost on
us, what do you think alleyway staircases smell like?

i guess you could
                    say
          you did bushopping

                              on samtrans.

REMEMBERING ORFN

from an indian reservation in the lower haight
fresh curses return to latex, to powder
illegal flute music

PAINTING ON THE FREEWAY

Painting on the freeway, cops pull up and I sling this heavy ass duffel bag
full of paint over my shoulder and we run, I make it home and light a joint
and get a call – you gotta come out and BOMB, a friend is in town from New
York and he's only around one night so I go out again, lugging around this
heavy ass duffel bag full of paint and before we put anything up, cops roll up.
I say, 'Don't run, we haven't done anything yet' but one guy was just deported
from Canada and he runs, so everybody runs, I hide inside a garbage can and
put the lid on top. The cops walk down the alley, kicking over every garbage
can and finally they kick over my can. They're like 'Oh shit! It's Oscar the
Grouch!' as I tumble out and they handcuff us and throw us in the back seat
of their squad car and the cops go across the street to the bar for a really
long time – like an hour and a half – come back dead drunk, bringing with
them the bartender. One guy holds me and the other cop clocks me hard in
the face and we're like Oh my God! They're going to kill us! The bartender
is snickering and they give us back our IDs but they're covered in paint, my
paint, from the duffel bag, and they're laughing, 'If you use some turpentine,
that'll come right out . . . mostly.' And they let us go and say, 'If we see you
out again tonight, we promise we are going to kill you.'

I WAS KILLED BY A VIETNAM VET

I was killed by a Vietnam vet on a dirt road
that hovers far above the Tenderloin
far up I heard the faint squishing sound
of the soft skulls of angels
tropical morphine rain exited through my nose
a leash around my neck
in the millisecond
after he was acquitted
in My Lai.

Meditate on this, as I have.

I saw the Vietnam vet was never taken in, arrested, nothing.
    My parents couldn't speak a word of English.
    I was still a teenager.

DISJECTA MEMBRA

On the bus
a sign reads:
   'assaulting a bus driver is a crime'
a mime conversation between siblings
  mouthing as if in asl
    'are you sure it's a baby and not

                a baby elephant?'

       my 1st solo ride
       was at around 10 years old
       on the same bus
       as Spock and Kirk
       when they traveled
       back in time
       to my precise era
       and location
       and knock out
       a punk rocker.

       The Columbus Ave bus
       past the colossal
       strip joints
       a narcotic odor
       of Chinese
       childhood

blinking
neon sex.

All childhood
is pulp.

DISJECTA MEMBRA 2

On a rooftop
halfway through
a toy
pissing in a can
of paint
stretching
it out
night time breeze
blowing a mist
of urine up into
my eyes.

CREATION MYTH

After the war the good people began to rebuild however building reminded
the good people of war fleets constructing atoms splitting farms ddt spray-
ing so instead the good people began to explore the immaterial spaces and
demolish notions that formerly trembled under their own weight and there
was a great hissing sound of deflation as if the world relaxed its bowels
all at once and there was awareness and relief and sensation for the first
time since before the war and the good people promised that to build was to
destroy and identity was a chimera and they all went vegetarian.

We are again at war building again and the architects of mayhem learned
from their mistake and now make weapons from words and other immaterial
resources and the architects are so woven with the people they are simulta-
neously one as steel requires water and the ultimate monument is that the
good people are hypnotized unaware there is even a war at all.

CLIMBING A METAL ROOF

Climbing a metal roof with p on a very cold night, roof was frozen and p slips on the ice and slides down and i'm laughing uncontrollably then fall on my ass and slide down the roof myself. p laughing and slips, slides down another level of the roof then i slip myself, again, until we slide down three levels of roof! then there's no more laughter, just moaning from the pain of slamming down on our asses. below us, on the sidewalk, a prostitute catches us and starts yelling, 'no free looks! no free looks!' over and over, blowing up our spot, 'no free looks! no free looks!' and there we are – stranded on the roof, in the freezing cold, helplessly unable to move from the pain of falling and this prostitute is yelling at us. just then out of nowhere, this guy comes out of the shadows of the sidewalk and punches her lights out, she falls to the ground cold and we're like (0) (0)

BIGFOOT

I met Bigfoot in San Rafael, of all places.
He told me he was temporarily living in Oakland
    I have no proof.

    Crackle in the forest
        pulley scraping cable
metallic squeal.

If I hadn't seen Bigfoot
in San Rafael,
    it wouldn't mean a thing
    for he has tremendous ears.
Mr mud closes his gaps while Mr sunsplash

              is distracted.

Ofcourse he is hairy all over,
save the bottoms of his gigantic feet.
He can fart whenever he pleases;
             his ass is a musical instrument.
(he came to Northern California decades ago from New Jersey to be in
proximity to music, which was and remains dead)

Bigfoot reminded me I was primal.
And hunters, don't bother looking for him –
    you smell like shit.

Especially in the concrete places,
squirting fangs of sorcery.

AT THE HARDWARE STORE

– Good morning fellas, how can I help you today?
– Hey man, we need a lot of paint!
– Great! Aisle 9. Follow me.
– Can you lift us down one of those giant drums of exterior house paint?
– No problem! What else?
– I don't know . . . Let's just fill up the shopping cart to be safe.
– Yes, just in case. Let's overflow the shopping cart all the way.
– Ok fellas! You got a big job ahead of you today?
– Yeah, a hella big job!
– Yeah! Thanks so much for your help, man!
– No problem! Good luck fellas!
– Have a nice day!
– See ya next time!

And we would walk right out the front door,
without stopping at the register,
sometimes up to three times a day,
cans rolling clang clang clang
out onto the street.

ODE

Vinegar footprints
in threads of BART train carpet,
how many fibers of your cloth benches
where a 14 year old once read
The Autobiography of Malcolm X
as once white stains turned before his eyes
royal purple as gum
as if the prince in
One Thousand and One Nights
willed this magic carpet
straight to the bottom of the Bay.
Since that your magic seat is tore up,
                    you are preserved.

A PUBLIC MURAL

Emma Goldman   dance of the hippopotamus to rattle open the prison gate.
Mahatma Ghandi   yarn-spinning to liberate the inner state.
Frantz Fanon   from behind a white mask, the third world knows.
José Martí   from behind a white rose, an apostle grows.
Dolores Huerta   beaten by sfpd but her stockton stock was too tough.
Lolita Lebrón   coming not to kill but die for love.
Archbishop Romero   eucharist bullets for the poor's pastor.
Pancho Villa   cockroach's triumph over the schoolmaster.
Martin Luther King   the voice that can carry.
Patrice Lumumba   freely elected by african dignity.
Augusto César Sandino   reign of the spirit of light and truth.
Leila Khaled   terror of exodus on the spirit of youth.
Sitting Bull   mystery and humor across native land.
Malcolm X   .completing the hajj across saudi sand.
Nelson Mandela   harmonious spear of the nation.
Zofia Yamaika   one armed teenager vs. nazi suffocation.
Frida Khalo   hoping never to return to this lonely place.
Maurice Bishop   the airport at the end of the rat race.
Souha Bechara   aerobics instructor turned assassin.
Che Guevara   beloved buddy and hungry argentinian.
Rachel Corrie   standing alone for another's home.
Leonard Peltier   doing time for the unknown.
Audre Lorde   inequality upon the axes of identity.
Edward Said   identity upon the falsehoods of oriental pity.
Aristide   haiti's heart exiled to a revolving glass door.
Farabundo Martí   one of thirty thousand lost at la matanza of el salvador.

Rigoberta Menchú   an uprooted maya testimonial.

César Chavez   striking the farm, striking a deal.

Judi Bari   in the shadow of the big tree.

Harriet Tubman   killing the snake by night for hundreds free.

Assata Shakur   now there's guns on both sides.

Madame Bình   revolution means nothing if not happiness provides.

Emiliano Zapata   the general's genderless ranks.

Marilyn Buck   prison dreams of pulverized capital from black-owned banks.

Rosa Luxemburg   the rich rubbed her out, may she rest in peace.

Joe Hill   nothing like a song for the spirit's release.

Mumia Abu-Jamal   along with his brother, refusing defense.

Bernadette Devlin   the troubles bullhorn talking sense.

WOULD YOU LIKE TO BUY AN OX?

Would you like to buy an ox?
Would you like to feed it paper?
Would you show him a good time?
Would you whack him with a stapler?

Would you share your bed with an ox?
Would you chop off all his legs?
Pit him against a burning rooster?
Singing doggerel til he begs?

Can an ox be folded?
Can an ox be melted?
Can an ox be seethed?
Can an ox be svelted?

How does it know it's a good day or a bad?
How does it know it's dead yet?
How does an ox rank churches?
How do you feel about this pet?
Would you like to buy an ox?

TEMPERANCE

Deep river, moving steady and slow
From within fish swim through the flow
Life-giving stream, from pole to pole
The symbol of total self-control
From the rainbow we gather all concept of color
An angel pours liquid from muller to muller
The wild horse of disorder couldn't drag me apart
From the water of Creation, Temperance and Art

Aloe and irises grow on the bank
Though serene, the mind does not draw a blank
But rather gives birth to the fruit of idea
Lost ships are guided into the marina
Tranquility is the word I was looking for
Because true Art never leaves you wanting more
From this place, everything starts
The water of Creation, Temperance and Art

Balanced are feathers that float down the rush
Steady is the hand upon flesh does touch
Some say Reason is the enemy of Design
I don't know about that, but both can combine
Like fire and water, two sides of a coin
To make the element of wind, their hands must join
Three elements, a trinity, hung over your heart:
The water of Creation, Temperance and Art

THE TRUCK DRIVER AND MALVERDE

On the mountains I was driving
a gigantic truck filled with traps
to rob the rich northerners
and return the loot to Sinaloa
where my mother was born

Straight heading to San Antonio
but first to be questioned
by a checkpoint puppet goverment
they too are criminals, but for the rich
in collusion with the Americans

They are waving my truck into the blockade
thinking they are so sexual
with their weapons outside their clothes
I also have guns, but not so foolish as to reveal
until it is my advantage to do so

As I approached the checkpoint, I was not scared
for around my neck was
an image of Jesús Malverde
surrounded by embroidered cardboard
I gave me a kiss and said a prayer
to protect me and my burden:

Malverde, I humbly ask a favor, spirit
(I placed a stone on his altar in Culiacán)
today I need your guide
to pass through this checkpoint
and deliver my burden to San Antonio

Malverde, who took from the rich
and delivered to the poor!
that has the same name as the Messiah
take care of me for a few minutes
and I will forever honor you

My truck came to an abrupt stop
the man with the gun asked my destination
San Antonio, because I do not need to lie
the man looked at me coldly in the eye
and he waved his hand at me to proceed

Malverde, blessed Saint of Sinaloa!
I kiss your image again!
and pray your spirit finds rest
on the other side of the legendary borderline
between evil and green

AN UNUSUAL ESCAPE

PHENOMENON OF GEOTHERMAL LITHIA WATER ERUPTION SAVES TRAPPED MINERS.

COPPEROPOLIS, NOVEMBER 13. – Yesterday morning, eight miners trapped fourteen hours in the Van Goading silt mine were awakened by a thrust upward to the surface by a fountain of groundwater. All eight miners arrived safely soaked wet. Samuel Ward, Prof. of Geology, Univ. of Cal., Berkeley, said the only previous known occurrence of this phenomenon was 1733, West Virginia, when the buried bodies from a township graveyard were showered upon the residences in that area.

.   .

this

graveyard

DIALOGUE OF THE SHADOW AND THE ECHO BELONGING TO SADE

A DUET

Shadow:
A child of Helios, cast by sunlight, I walk alongside the Marquis
Though sometimes I follow him, other times he follows me!

Echo:
Wonderful! Let me show you what you've just said:
'I lead, I follow, I am a friend,' would you rather instead
Hear me mock our master, when he's in distress
Shouting for help to the valley below, a bloody mess
His leg broken, or belly poisoned by doll's eyes
His voice echoing on the canyon walls, mocking his cries

Shadow:
Boring echo! Don't you ever shut up?
The curse of man's tongue is to interrupt
We, the family of light, see shades with equal weight
And if the Marquis were to fall, thus would be his fate

Echo:
Okay, shadow, then let us suppose
The Marquis were writing, in a state of repose
Would he not imagine his voice speaking back at him?
For, in writing, one's inner-voice sings like a hymn
And the Marquis puts it down only after, to the page

Therefore, because of me, he is a legend throughout the age
I am the voice, born of intellect
A writer knows to show me the proper respect
The writer is my dog, I reveal him his shortcomings
Like singing to oneself a tune, whistling, or humming
I voice the guttural, yes, but most of all I mimic
That your 'fate,' even consciousness itself, is just a gimmick

Shadow:
If death were not certain, I would say you were right
But even the voice fades without light
For all things come from it, and also it's lacking
Evil is cast by virtue's tracking
When the Marquis was a boy and he grew in height
I, his Shadow, grew the same, aright
For virtue and evil, both are born of the same source
The Marquis knows this best of all, of course
Death, the great shadow, can even eclipse you
I can even cheat the devil his due

Echo:
While you are eclipsing insects and puny wildflowers,
The eternal word, which came first, showers
Like the Pentecost, mankind, with doubt and dung
Causing them to speak in a strange, unknown tongue

Shadow:
Man sees himself through the scope of history
Herein lies the great mystery

That the lessons of the past safeguard today
Through foreshadowing, the prophetic way
And man, seeing it coming, avoids the curse
Therefore, my friend, the shadow came first!

Echo:
The louder man shouts, the more his voice will echo
Needing this depth to feel, to learn, and to grow
The single-dimension that you reflect
Leads man to use words like 'great,' which I reject
Being is more subtle, a sham, your 'mystery'
And in my opinion, the Marquis would agree!

BY DECREE OF EMPEROR NORTON

By decree of Emperor Norton
there will be a road to the Farallones
that people may begin trade relations
with the great colony of seabirds

By decree of Emperor Norton
protector of Mexico
inventor of the bridge to Oakland
let the Chinese be!

By decree of Emperor Norton
a twenty-five dollar fine
to loquacious newcomers
effusing the word 'frisco'

By decree of Emperor Norton
may he and his two dogs
Bummer and Lazarus
dine for free at the finest city restaurants

By decree of Emperor Norton
may his papal dress remain blanched
his beaver hat perennially fluffy
set with fresh peacock feather and rosette

By decree of Emperor Norton
a pardon to the offending officer
for false arrest of the monarch
on suspicion of mafficking

No harm done, however
the police are fine men and women
who patrol these city streets
paved with trash and guns

By decree of Emperor Norton
may no good dog ever die
especially not the Emperor's
so, rise, Lazarus, rise!

A FREE SONG

This song is free
I mean it doesn't cost a thing
And you can't buy it
Because it's not for sale

This song is worthless
Got no practical value, no msrp
And it could easily disappear forever
Because it is free

Fulfills no vital purpose
Doesn't earn anybody a single dollar
And if it was never sung a second time
Nobody would care

And that's free
Free as can be
Free from all money
Free Free Free

When there's nothing to manufacture
Then there's nothing to defend
And you won't need to be starting war
Because you'd be free

This song says nothing about anything
Because there's nothing worthwhile
To sing about when you have nothing to prove
And nobody to fool

Don't even need to try being free
It's easier than breathing
As easy as turning around
In a world where everything is in motion

WITH DEATH COMES A CHOICE

A good man was about to die and Satan saw that St. Peter had already writ the good man's name in the great book of the constellations, so Satan decided to plan some mischief. He contrived to bribe Death to tempt the good man. How does one bribe Death? Satan promised to restore his face; to add flesh where there is only skull. An impossibility, of course. Death was fooled and agreed to the task, making haste for Earth, imagining what color eyes would adorn his new face, whether his hair would be curly or straight or if he would remain bald. The dying man lay in bed alone, meditating on his life, while his three faithful daughters, who were old now too, cried on the other side of the door (moments before he had kissed them goodbye and asked to let him die alone and in peace).

Death appeared by the good man's bedside. The time had come to cross the Great River. Death, following Satan's instruction, offered the wise old man a choice.

DEATH: As reward for living such a generous and humble life, you are allowed to bring to the next world one attribute from this world. For we know the next world is not like this world; this token will remind you that your life was not in vain. You may choose to keep either Consciousness, Intellect, Time, or Personality. Now which will it be?

The suffering man was not delirious, but listened closely, gazing into the void of the talking skull's eye, mouth and nasal cavities.

THE GOOD MAN: What you offer is a trick, for each of these things from this world is useless without the other. Without Intellect, Consciousness is formless building. Without Time, Intellect has no progress. Personality, least of all, will have worth in the next world, for I could not appreciate it without Consciousness, I could not refine it without Intellect, and without the unflinching hand of Time, my Personality would grow lazy, and I would be obliged to carry around this meat-self like a pet, a lame dog I am too cowardly to euthanize. No, I decline the choice. Take me to Beulah, where I may kiss the wounds of Jesus!

When Death realized he was deceived and would never receive his face, he vanished to search the underworld for retribution from Satan. And although the good man chose correctly, which was not to choose at all, when he finally died, he was not awarded any more in Heaven than entrance.

PAPERCLIP WHEN SCIENCE EVOLVES

who makes the we can what elves can make science evolve mucking in the
what horrible and salty and definitely not normal sometimes magical but
mostly a jungled mess by anything and everything skiffle honey rum springa
memories behind decapitated narration of where now we're skiffling or
what science may evolve to be, the decapitated head that still talks soplano
for the seven points of the magnetic one north or what is north to you and
west where we enter the circle from roving bards standing with the local
bard south our brothers and sisters across the ancient big rio rolling with
the sound of stone plates kissing like whales made of black swirling quartz
eastward both twilights' gateway between worlds the pickled sphinx purrs
like a bent back paperclip if sphinx purr both twilights' gateway is a place up
to the sky people where there's a star for you the star falling to the mother
and dead homies alike to keep us in check for our real earthen foot and
infernal regions and humorously not concluding in the seventh point which
is yourself and out again at the speed of what is not timed for the wheel
stops for only one reason and thank the multitude of heavens there is no
reason to stop but a wheel and star and a skiffle and whatever the hell else
you got on you to throw in the cauldron our spleen of water flavored by a
strawberry bloodline from the future and thank the children there is music
bursting from the falls twinkling and all body parts yet unknown when
science evolves

LAST DAY OF JUNE

Last day of June
sleepfishing with
a better woman
on the longest night of the year
    our dream
of mountain water in the Nile
and nothing more.

No, nothing more.
We have peaches
    coming out of our ears.
We have conflict.
We have sweetness.

What more, of what more
could we sleepfish?
Except of more June,
more sanity and also insanity,
just not the fried monotony
of late Summer
miles-long blackberry bushes in Ukiah
bleak Fall, my birthday
and another year
    no . . . please, more June.

GROUCH BAG

Pay your dues and break a leg. I broke both my own legs dancing Vaudeville as Chairman of the Teamsters Union. The doctor put me in a squint – never trust an optometrist to do serious work. Ready for the next stage, I rode shot-gun west through Indian Territory, but unable to speak Sanskrit, I turned around and rode chakra east. I rode from Labor Day to Halloween, then I rode broomstick, making a clean sweep of my ex-wife's assets. Or was it her my assets? I can't remember witch, thank odd. Alimony never! But dues always on the last day of the month. Have I paid my dues? Huh! I got the scars to prove it. I paid dues all the way from Cheyenne to Chattanooga, now it's my turn to live out my golden years. Yes, my golden years – for I wasn't just the Chairman of the Teamsters, I was also the Treasurer and make no qualms about spending other people's dues, it's my solemn duty. So long, suckers! Save your qualms for the poor! Ah, those old honky-tonk monkey-shines . . . I was just wondering, has a cannibal ever written a book? Once, I was taken in by a literate cannibal society. When I finally had to leave the village they told me to 'eat a leg.' I remember those hot nights in the jungle reading the classics that I might get drowsy, the upside to insomnia. Reading the big book looking for a loophole. I learned enough to learn I know nothing but somehow still suffer the fool. Pardon my French – it's a beautiful language, French.

The four humors are blood, phlegm, black bile & yellow bile,
                                                    but who am I?

DESERT SUNDOWN

That slow desert sundown
Like it don't ever want to go down . . .

Our brakes went out in Gallup, NM
the mechanic at Pep Boys said it would take five days
but the first day was not a day, because it was a Sunday
    'It takes a couple days to get a new axle
    from probably Albuquerque,' he said.
F that – we went looking for a second opinion.
Only the finest fast food
Denny's A+ good coffee
Stoned at Applebees, made me uptight.
At the motel, baseball on TV – gotta get back into baseball. I believed I
noticed a wider strikezone, in favor of the pitcher, a welcome change after the
past decade of batter domination. Younger game now, kids are made tough.
Saw a beaner bounce right off the guy's arm the way popcorn falls off a movie
theater balcony onto a head below.

Favorite players from back in the day:
Rickey Henderson
Tony Gwynn
Will Clark
Kevin Mitchell
Robby Thompson
Matt Williams
Dave Stewart

Dennis Eckersley
Darryl Strawberry
Jose Canseco
Mark McGwire
Carney Lansford
Bo Jackson
Mike Schmidt
Orel Hershiser
Ken Griffey Jr.
Reggie Jackson
Wade Boggs
Roger Clemens
Cal Ripken Jr.
Doc Gooden
Rock Raines
Nolan Ryan
Randy Johnson
Greg Maddux
Dave Winfield
Barry Bonds
Andre Dawson

Favorite players from the old school:
Willie Mays
Willie McCovey
Joe DiMaggio
Pete Rose
Babe Ruth
Hank Aaron

Roberto Clemente
Rod Carew
Sandy Koufax
Ty Cobb
Walter Johnson
Shoeless Joe Jackson
Mickey Mantle
Roger Maris
Carl Yastrzemski
Harmon Killebrew
Johnny Bench
Mel Ott
Bob Gibson
Satchel Paige
Warren Spahn
Ted Williams
Lou Gehrig
Jackie Robinson
Orlando Cepeda

Great baseball names:
Catfish Hunter
Rollie Fingers
Oil Can Boyd
Yogi Berra
Angel Pagan
Dizzy Dean
Dusty Baker
Chipper Jones

Ripper Collins
Pee Wee Reese
Howard Johnson

This is the diary of a nitwit, a happy fool.
Saw a couple prairie dogs peekin' out their holes,
    a bunch of hares too hoppin' in the grass and sand.

I wish ESPN added the players' names when they're onscreen.
Desert trash near newberry springs
    a pile of tires, pile of rocks
    bebop on the van stereo.
We buried h at a rest area under the biggest tree. Maybe dig it up next time
I'm passing through.
How many years or months or days or hours would it take for my body to
decompose in a place like this?
Let me decompose a poem for you . . .

    take your time going east
    the 40 to needles, flagstaff
    the brakes go out in gallup, nm

We brought the van to a guy named Richard
Who said he could do the fix.

ARTISANAL PORNOGRAPHY

Beginning with the Audre Lorde poem,
                    'Who Said It Was Simple'
And ending with a recipe for
Brown butter cherry clafoutis.

AND WHEN I DEPARTED

And when I departed
I left behind a debt
for all my possessions
were buried along with me
similar to how sailors
are always buried
wearing their sea-hats
an item as personal
as any part of their body
on the presumption
all this personal stuff
would prove useful
when I would awaken
to the cold blast
of the other side
having known
our saturated times
would never be
monumental
in any way.

A MONK'S HABIT

'We live in a black hole'
a monk sings to a knot in a tree.

'We are not always defined by acts'
the monk sings to a falling nut.

'This song is as temporary as the string's vibration.
We are not defined by faith, we are not defined at all.
        But enough fog!
Ships only emerge from fog, there is never submersion.
That is, if a ship is lost, no one will ever hear of it.
Therefore, if you are talking of a ship, it has emerged.
Now, vessel sail to my hand!
Let's drink!'

What lifts a monks daydreams?
is a monk already retired?

Pities women that they should burden a child
disgust, admiration,
        the stuff of love songs
however the monk doesn't sing love songs
his art is of sacred prostitution
&the holy debauch
lower, to enlightenment
and above all a ganges of booze

wonderful beer until the fatal glass
wildflowers birdsong
          &booze
our monastery is a distillery
our tradition places booze at christ's first miracle
                              water to wine
drinking outdoors not in some windowless tavern
we sleep where we fall down certain months

Singing drinking
sometimes softly weeping
agony   a great many songs

This mutant world.
It is mutant because it is fragile,
like women.

A Life Without
without glory   bah, glory.
without money   money's trash.
without women   never.
without song   that's no life.

Life is hard & long
long & hard is life
(with admiration for the Goliard)

THANK YOU CODERS

Thank you coders for your meddleyarn swigossip and virilatin statistrips.
Thank you for this magneticape wrung round found under streaming
overpast.

Thanks for compatriotshop. you
    bring hoy. new
    fearleast obsane
    scienterrific
    slades
    of numerologics,
wonderfurry psyoptic

                  fleece and

    false fags
Thank you codders for
the cod.

You are matte.

A PRAYER

We dance for those who cannot dance.
We sing for those who cannot sing.
We dance for those who are incarcerated.
We dance for the injured
                          and the afflicted.
For the addict. For the homeless.
The castigated. The impugned.
The accused. The misrepresented.
We dance for the men and women in uniform.
We dance for the loved ones who are traveling.
We dance for the loved ones who have gone before us.
We dance for the loved ones who are missing.
We dance for the loved ones who are lost.
We dance for those who are yet to dance.
We dance not for those who can dance.
We dance not for ourselves.

Feng Shui in the Old West.
Billy the Kid was shot in the head
   due to poor bed placement.

STOCK SONG 1

He steals raw meat from Safeway,
and claiming it is rotten, returns it for cash.
    He is LaVeyan.

STOCK SONG 2

Thus she came into her possession
a brand new computer, for a barter.
    She is a foot fetish girl.

STOCK SONG 3

Write a stock song.
Tell me a v long story.
Like this:
Men she finds on the computer pay $200 for her
    to kick them in the genitals.

STOCK SONG 4

Let's recall our individual lives, just before
we were married:
>   I was a fiend,
>   you were a foot fetish girl.

Meanwhile, in NYC . . .

She shot up in the bathroom
in the Egyptian wing at the Met
and walked into a mirror.

                '   .

text / illustrations   Cass McCombs

design   John Brian King
author photograph   Silvia Grav
title page lettering   Greg Gardner
printed by   SYL / Barcelona

ISBN: 978-1-943679-10-2

published by Spurl Editions

Spurl Editions
www.spurleditions.com